KU-062-870

WINCHESTER
DISCOVERY
CENTRE
0845 603 5631

WITHDRAWN

CL.69(02/06.)

C003765075

This book is due for return on or before the last date shown
above: it may, subject to the book not being reserved by
another reader, be renewed by personal application, post, or
telephone, quoting this date and details of the book.

HAMPSHIRE COUNTY COUNCIL   100%
County Library   recycled paper
PERF A.

Music compiled by Peter Evans and Peter Lavender
Song background notes by Michael Kennedy

Text edited by Pearce Marchbank

Book design by Pearce Marchbank and Ben May
Text and image research by Katie Cornford

Printed in the United Kingdom by
Page Bros Ltd, Norwich, Norfolk

...lusive Distributors:
...sic Sales Limited
...Frith Street,
...don W1V 5TZ, England.
...sic Sales Pty Limited
...Rothschild Avenue,
...sebery, NSW 2018,
...stralia.

...der No. AM944163
...N 0-7119-6598-6
...s book © Copyright 1998
...Wise Publications

...authorised reproduction of any part of
...publication by any means including
...tocopying is an infringement of copyright.

...e photographs used in this book are from
...hives of contemporary sources, and are
...ieved to be in the public domain. As it has not
...en possible to trace the owners of any images
...ch may still remain in copyright, we would be
...teful therefore if the photographers or owners
...cerned would contact us.

...his publication is not authorised for sale in
...e United States of America and/or Canada

...ur **Guarantee of Quality**
...publishers, we strive to produce every book
...he highest commercial standards.
...s book has been carefully designed to minimise
...kward page turns and to make playing from
...real pleasure.
...ticular care has been given to specifying acid-free,
...tral-sized paper made from pulps which have not
...n elemental chlorine bleached. This pulp is from
...ned sustainable forests and was produced with
...cial regard for the environment.
...roughout, the printing and binding have been
...nned to ensure a sturdy, attractive publication
...ch should give years of enjoyment.
...ur copy fails to meet our high standards,
...ase inform us and we will gladly replace it.

...sic Sales' complete catalogue describes thousands
...itles and is available in full colour sections by
...ject, direct from Music Sales Limited.
...ase state your areas of interest and send a
...que/postal order for £1.50 for postage to:
...sic Sales Limited, Newmarket Road, Bury St.
...munds, Suffolk IP33 3YB.

...t the Internet Music Shop at
...p://www.musicsales.co.uk

Wise Publications
London/New York/Paris/Sydney/Copenhagen/Madrid

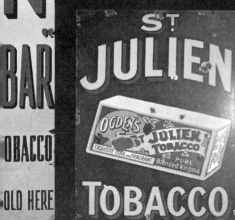

It is better to be making the news than taking it; to be an actor rather than a critic.
WINSTON CHURCHILL
(RIGHT) MATA HARI, EROTIC DANCER AND GERMAN SPY, EXECUTED 1917

'The unsinkable Titanic'.
ADVERTISEMENT, 1912.
(LEFT) THE TITANIC AND HER SISTER SHIP THE OLYMPIC UNDER CONSTRUCTION IN BELFAST IN 1910

Terminological inexactitude.
WINSTON CHURCHILL

I'm just going outside and I may be some time.
CAPTAIN LAWRENCE OATES' LAST WORDS ON SCOTT'S ILL-FATED 1912 EXPEDITION TO THE SOUTH POLE (RIGHT)

Nothing in life is so exhilirating in life as to be shot at without result.
WINSTON CHURCHILL.
(ABOVE) ONE OF CHURCHILL'S BEST-SELLING BOOKS OF THE 1910's

HAMPSHIRE COUNTY LIBRARY

784.3 | 0711965986

ou can tell the ideals of a
tion by it's advertisements.
ORMAN DOUGLAS, 1917.
CING PAGE) ENAMEL STREET
VERTISING SIGNS c.1910

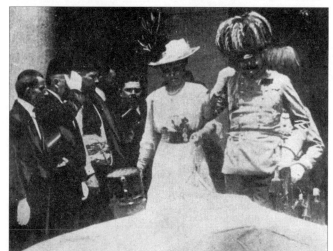

Assasination is the extreme form of censorship.

GEORGE BERNARD SHAW, IN 'MAN AND SUPERMAN', 1903. (LEFT) ARCHDUKE FERDINAND JUST BEFORE HIS ASSASINATION IN SARAJEVO, JUNE 1914: THE ACT THAT TRIGGERED THE FIRST WORLD WAR

I am not a criminal, for I destroyed a bad man. I thought it was right.

GAVRILO PRINCECIP, THE ASSASIN

The lamps are going out all over Europe; we shall not see them lit again in our lifetime.

EDWARD, VISCOUNT GREY, 1914 (ABOVE) A 1915 RECRUITING POSTER; CONSCRIPTION BECAME COMPULSORY THE NEXT YEAR

Armed neutrality is ineffectual enough at best... the world must be made safe for democracy.

WOODROW WILSON, 1917. (BELOW) THE PARIS PEACE CONFERENCE, 1919: LLOYD GEORGE OF ENGLAND, ORLANDO OF ITALY, CLEMENCEAU OF FRANCE AND WOODROW WILSON OF THE USA

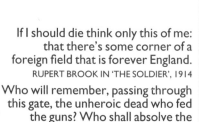

If I should die think only this of me: that there's some corner of a foreign field that is forever England.

RUPERT BROOK IN 'THE SOLDIER', 1914

Who will remember, passing through this gate, the unheroic dead who fed the guns? Who shall absolve the foulness of their fate, those doomed, conscripted, unvictorious ones?

SIEGFRIED SASSOON IN 'ON PASSING THE NEW MENIN GATE', 1918 (RIGHT) THE MENIN ROAD, 1917

Peace is not only better than war but infinitely more arduous.

GEORGE BERNARD SHAW, 1918

"Votes for Women," November 26, 1915.

Registered at the G.P.O. as a Newspaper.

The War Paper for Women

VOTES FOR WOMEN

OFFICIAL ORGAN OF THE UNITED SUFFRAGISTS

VOL. IX. (Third Series), No. 403. FRIDAY, NOVEMBER 26, 1915. Price 1d. Weekly (Post Free 1½d.)

VOTES FOR HEROINES AS WELL AS HEROES

CHIVALRY: "Men and women protect one another in the hour of death. With the addition of the woman's vote, they would be able to protect one another in life as well."

Women upset everything.
GEORGE BERNARD SHAW,
IN 'PYGMALION', 1912

A woman is only a woman,
but a good cigar is a smoke.
RUDYARD KIPLING IN
'THE BETROTHED'

The female of the species is
more deadly than the male.
RUDYARD KIPLING IN
'THE FEMALE OF THE SPECIES'

There is no 'female mind'.
The brain is not an organ of sex.
As well speak of a 'female liver'.
CHARLOTTE PERKINS GILLMAN
IN 'WOMEN AND ECONOMICS'

Women are growing honester,
braver, stronger, more beautiful
and skillful and able and free,
more human in all ways.
CHARLOTTE PERKINS GILLMAN
IN 'WOMEN AND ECONOMICS'

Genius is one per cent inspiration and ninety-nine per cent perspiration!
THOMAS EDISON; INVENTOR OF THE GRAMOPHONE (RIGHT), THE ELECTRIC LIGHT, THE ELECTRIC RAILWAY, MOTION PICTURES... (ABOVE, LEFT) WITH HIS THREE FAMOUS INVENTOR FRIENDS: FORD, BURROUGHS AND FIRESTONE

Ah! Sweet Mystery Of Life

Music by Victor Herbert
Words by Rida Johnson Young

© Copyright 1910 M. Witmark & Sons, USA.
B. Feldman & Company Limited, 127 Charing Cross Road, London WC2.
All Rights Reserved. International Copyright Secured.

Irish born composer Victor Herbert found musical success in America. His operetta Naughty Marietta (1910), written with lyricist Rida Johnson Young, was set in New Orleans in 1780. The vivacious heroine Marietta promises to marry whoever can finish the melody of a certain song. That man is dashing Captain Richard, the song 'Ah! Sweet Mystery Of Life'.

hopes, the joy and i-dle tears that fall!_____ For 'tis love, and love a-lone, the world is

seek - ing; And 'tis love, and love a-lone, that can re - pay, 'tis the

ans - wer, 'tis the end and all of liv-ing,_____ for it is

love a - lone that rules for aye! For 'tis

love, and love a-one, the world is seek - ing, for 'tis love, and love a-lone, that can re-

-pay! 'tis the ans - wer, 'tis the end and all of

liv ing,____ for it is love a - lone that rules for aye!____

William Henry Crump was better known as top-of-the-bill music hall artiste Harry Champion who specialised in songs about food and drink. However, even he couldn't resist the 1911 showstopper 'Any Old Iron'. The song was resurrected for use during the Second World War to encourage the collection of scrap metal and railings.

Any Old Iron

Music by Charles Collins
Words by Fred Terry & A. E. Sheppard

© Copyright 1911 Herman Darewski Music Publishing Company, 127 Charing Cross Road, London WC2.
All Rights Reserved. International Copyright Secured.

1. Just a week or two a-go my poor old Un-cle Bill, went and kick'd the buck-et and he
(Verses 2 - 4 see block lyric)

left me in his will. The oth-er day I popp'd a-round to see poor Aun-tie Jane, she

would-n't give you tup-pence for your old watch chain, old i-ron, old i-ron?" i-ron?'

Verse 2:
I went to the City once and thought I'd have a spree
The Mayor of London, he was there, that's who I went to see
He dashed up in a canter, with a carriage and a pair
I shouted "Holler boys" and threw my hat up in the air.

Just then the Mayor he began to smile
Saw my face and then he shouted "Lummy what a dial!"
Started a Lord Mayoring and I thought that I should die
When pointing to my watch and chain he holler'd to me "Hi!"

Verse 3:
Just to have a little bit of fun the other day
Made up in my watch and chain I went and drew my pay
Then got out with a lot of other Colonels "on the loose"
I got full right up to here in fourp'ny "stagger juice."

One of them said "We want a pot of ale
"Run him to the ragshop, and we'll bung him on the scale"
I heard the fellow say "What's in this bundle that you've got"
Then whisper to me kindly: "Do you want to lose your lot?"

Verse 4:
Shan't forget when I got married to Selina Brown
The way the people laugh'd at me, it made me feel a clown
I began to wonder, when their dials began to crack
If by mistake I'd got my Sunday trousers front to back.

I wore my chain on my darby kell
The sun was shining on it and it made me look a swell
The organ started playing and the bells began to ring
My chain began to rattle, so the choir began to sing.

First sung by Eddie Miller and Helen Vincent at the Garden Cafe in New York in 1911, 'Alexander's Ragtime Band' was an early hit for composer Irving Berlin. It was sung by Ethel Merman in the film of the same name - and Johnie Ray in There's No Business Like Show Business, Britain first heard the song in the revue Hello Ragtime, which starred Lew Hearn and Shirley Kellogg.

Alexander's Ragtime Band

Words & Music by Irving Berlin

© Copyright 1911 Irving Berlin Music Corporation, USA.
B. Feldman & Company Limited, 127 Charing Cross Road, London WC2.
All Rights Reserved. International Copyright Secured.

1. Oh, ma hon - ey, oh, ma hon - ey, bet - ter hur - ry and
(Verse 2 see block lyric)

Verse 2:
Oh, ma honey, oh, ma honey
There's a fiddle with notes that screeches
Like a chicken, like a chicken
And the clarinet, is a colored pet
Come and listen, come and listen
To a classical band what's peaches
Come now, some how
Better hurry along.

Blues My Naughty Sweetie Gives To Me

Words & Music by Arthur N. Swanstrom,
Charles R. McGarron & Carey Morgan

© Copyright 1919 Jos W. Stern & Company, USA.
Assigned to Edward B. Marks Music Company, USA.
Campbell Connelly & Company Limited, 8/9 Frith Street, London W1.
All Rights Reserved. International Copyright Secured.

Although a prolific songwriter, Arthur Swanstrom's greatest and most enduring hit was 'Blues My Naughty Sweetie Gives To Me', written in cahoots with Charles R. McGarron and Carey Morgan. From its first appearance in 1919 it quickly became a jazz standard, memorably recorded by Jimmy Noone and Ted Lewis and his orchestra.

1. What is that song a-bout kiss-es? What is that song a-bout

(Verse 2 see block lyric)

smiles? If I could have— my way, I'd sing a song— to-day,

that would beat them all by miles, I would-n't sing— a-bout

smil - ing,——— that's not the ti - tle I'd choose,

I would sing— a-bout what I've got,— and what I've got's the wea-ry blues. There are

Chorus 2:

There are blues that you get when single
Those are blues that will give you pain
And there are blues when you're lonely
For your one and only
The blues you can never explain
There are blues that you get from longing
To hold someone on your knee
But the kind of blues that always stabs
Comes from hiring taxicabs
The blues my naughty sweetie gives to me.

Verse 2:

No use in chasing those rainbows
Rainbows will never help you
They look so bright and gay
But they will fade away
Then you'll find the sky's all blue
Look at the ocean and that's blue
My sweetie's eyes are blue too
When she got me she blew away
And natur'ly that makes me blue.

Chorus 3:

There are blues that you get from sweetie
When she 'phones to another guy
And there are blues when your honey
Spends all of your money
And blues when she tells you a lie
There are blues that you get when married
Wishing that you could be free
But the kind of blues that's good and blue
Comes from buying wine for two
The kind of blues my sweetie gives to me.

Don't Dilly Dally On The Way

Words & Music by Fred W. Leigh & Charles Collins

© Copyright 1997 Dorsey Brothers Music Limited, 8/9 Frith Street, London W1.
All Rights Reserved. International Copyright Secured.

The composer of 'Any Old Iron', Charles Collins, combined with the lyricist of 'Waiting At The Church', Fred Leigh, to write in 1915 the definitive song about moving house which became a favourite of the queen of the music hall, Marie Lloyd. It is also known by its first line - 'My Old Man Said "Follow The Van"'.

Moderato

ad lib.

1. We had to move a-way, 'cos the rent we could-n't pay, the

(Verses 2 & 3 see block lyrics)

24

got in-side all we could get in - side, _____ then we

packed all we could pack on the tail - board at the back, till there

was - n't a - ny room for me to ride. _____

My old man said, "Fol - low the van, don't dil - ly

dal - ly on the way!" Off went the cart with the

home packed in it, I walked be - hind with my old cock

lin - net. But I dil - lied and dal - lied, dal - lied and dil - lied,

lost the van and don't know where to roam.

1. I
2. Now
3. You

fz *p*

27

stopp'd on the way to have the old half - quart - ern, and I can't find
who's go - ing to put up the old iron bed - stead, if I can't find
can't trust the "spe-cials" like the old - time "cop- pers" when you can't find

1.

my way home.
my way home?
your way home.

2.

D.%.

home.
home?
home.

Verse 2:

I gave a helping hand with the marble wash-hand-stand,
And straight, we wasn't getting on so bad
All at once the carman bloke had an accident and broke
Well, the nicest bit of china that we had.

You'll understand of course, I was cross about the loss
Same as any other human woman would
But I soon got over that, what with"two-out" and a chat
'Cos it's little things like that what does you good.

Verse 3:

Oh! I'm in such a mess– I don't know the new address–
Don't even know the blessed neighbourhood
And I feel as if I might have to stay out all the night
And that ain't a-goin' to do me any good.

I don't make no complaint, but I'm coming over faint
What I want now is a good substantial feed
And I sort o' kind o' feel, if I don't soon have a meal
I shall have to rob the linnet of his seed.

I'll Take You Home Again Kathleen

Words & Music by Thomas P. Westendorf

© Copyright 1997 Dorsey Brothers Music Limited, 8/9 Frith Street, London W1.
All Rights Reserved. International Copyright Secured.

Although it sounds like an authentic Irish ballad, 'I'll Take You Home Again Kathleen' was written in either Indiana or Kentucky (the composer moved around a lot) by Thomas P. Westendorf. He wrote the song to comfort his wife who wanted to return to the East Coast. Her name, incidentally, was Jennie!

1. I'll take you home again, Kath-leen,
(Verses 2 & 3 see block lyrics)
a-cross the o-cean wild and wide, to

where your heart has ev - er been, since first you were my bon - ny bride. The ro - ses all have left your cheek, I've watched them fade a - way and die; your voice is sad when-e'er you speak, and tears be - dim your lov - ing eyes. Oh!

Verse 2:

I know you love me, Kathleen dear
Your heart was ever fond and true
I always feel when you are near
That life holds nothing dear but you.

The smiles that once you gave to me
I scarcely ever see them now
Though many, many times I see
A dark'ning shadow on your brow.

Verse 3:

To that dear home beyond the sea
My Kathleen shall again return
And when thy old friends welcome thee
Thy loving heart will cease to yearn.

Where laughs the little silver stream
Beside your mother's humble cot
And brightest rays of sunshine gleam
There all your grief will be forgot.

Fred Murray wrote this splendidly unsubtle music hall success in 1910. It was both sung and recorded by Harry Champion, born in Shoreditch and always a full blooded performer, who specialised in singing his songs at terrific speed. He continued to perform right into his seventies.

Ginger, You're Balmy

Words & Music by Fred Murray

© Copyright 1910 Francis Day & Hunter Limited, 127 Charing Cross Road, London WC2.
All Rights Reserved. International Copyright Secured.

1. I'm al-ways in the fash-ion, I'm a not-ed chap for that, so
(Verses 2 & 3 see block lyric)

late-ly I've been walk-ing a-bout the streets with-out a hat. I do with-out a ca-dy, and it

saves me half a quid. I'm like a bloom - ing sauce - pan on the fire with-out a lid.

I go you know, strol - ling round the town, and wag my lit - tle cane a -

- bout. Girls they all say "Gin - ger's on the mash!" Then

dig me in the ribs and loud - ly shout,

"Don't walk a-bout with-out your ca-dy on; Gin-ger, you're balm-y! Get your hair cut!" they all be-gin to cry. "With noth-ing on your nap-per, oh, you are a pie! Pies must have a lit-tle bit of crust, why don't you join the ar-my? If you

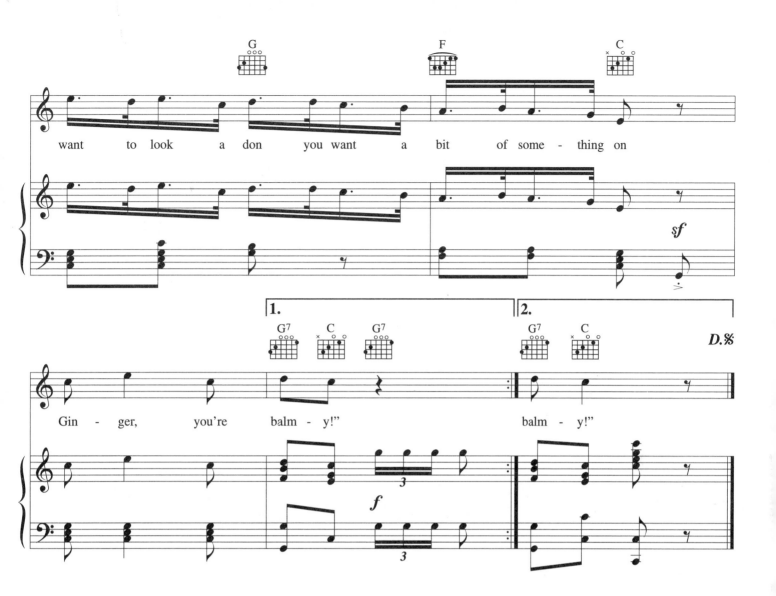

want to look a don you want a bit of some - thing on

1.

Gin - ger, you're balm - y!"

2.

balm - y!"

D.%

Verse 2:

One day I went into the zoo with such a smiling face
But, oh! there was a hullabaloo when I got in the place
The keeper started chasing me, though I was in a rage
They put a chain around my neck and bunged me in a cage.

I cried, "I'm not a monkey, on my word!"
Then I had to buy them all some beer
When they let me out they told me this
"If you want to keep away from here:"

Verse 3:

My missus took me in a pub; the guv'nor, Mister Hogg
He stroked my head and gave me a cake, he took me for a dog
A p'liceman stopped the traffic, shouted out with all his might
"Look out! here comes the North Pole with the top part all alight."

My wife said, "Your napper's like a sieve
"It's full of little holes I bet!
"When it rains 'twill let the water in
"And then your feet will both of 'em get wet."

35

If You Were The Only Girl In The World

American composer Nat D. Ayer came to Britain with the American Ragtime Octette in 1910 and stayed on to write a stream of hits. In 1916 he wrote 'If You Were The Only Girl In The World' for the London revue The Bing Boys Are Here, starring Violet Loraine. It has remained one of the most beloved of all show songs.

Music by Nat D. Ayer
Words by Clifford Grey

© Copyright 1916 B. Feldman & Company Limited, 127 Charing Cross Road, London WC2 (50%)/
Redwood Music Limited, Iron Bridge House, 3 Bridge Approach, London NW1 (50%).
All Rights Reserved. International Copyright Secured.

we could go on lov - ing in the same old way. A

Gar - den of E - - den just made for two, with

noth - ing to mar our joy,_____

I would say such won-der-ful things to you,

Lily Of Laguna

Words & Music by Leslie Stuart

© Copyright 1898 Francis Day & Hunter Limited, 127 Charing Cross Road, London WC2.
All Rights Reserved. International Copyright Secured.

Leslie Stuart wrote his greatest success for the blackface singer Eugene Stratton (a precursor of Al Jolson) who first performed 'Lily Of Laguna' at the Oxford Music Hall in 1898. Laguna, according to its composer, is on the road from New Orleans to California, a hundred miles to the left. Errol Flynn sang the ditty in Lilacs In The Spring. The original lyrics to this song may be considered racially insensitive; however, they have been included for historical authenticity.

Moderato

1. It's de same old tale of a pal-pa-ta-ting nig-gar ev-'ry
(Verse 2 see block lyric)

time, ev-'ry time; it's de same old

Verse 2:

When I first met Lil it was down in old Laguna at de dance, oder night
So she says, "Say, a'm curious for to know
"When ye leave here de way yer goin' to go
"'Kase a wants to see who de lady is dat claims ye all way home, way home tonight."

I says, "I've no gal, never had one,"
And den ma Lilly, ma Lilly, ma Lilly gal!
She says, kern't believe ye, a kern't believe ye
Else I'd like to have ye shapperoon me.

Dad says he'll esscortch me, says he'll esscortch me
But it's mighty easy for to lose him"
Since then each sun down I wander down here and roam around
Until I know ma lady wants me
Till I hear de music ob de signal sound.

This optimistic 1917 song, full of bravado, by John J. Stamford and Shamus O'Connor, has long been a favourite. It featured in two films: I'll Get By, which starred Dennis Day, a singer who made a speciality of 'Irish' songs, and Bad Lands Of Dakota, a Western with Robert Stack and Ann Rutherford.

MacNamara's Band

Words by John J. Stamford
Music by Shamus O'Connor

© Copyright 1917 Edwin Ashdown Limited, 8/9 Frith Street, London W1.
All Rights Reserved. International Copyright Secured.

1. My name is Mac-na-ma-ra, I'm the lead-er of the band, and tho' we're small in num-ber we're the best in all the land! Oh!

I am the con-duc-tor and we oft-en have to play with all the best mu-

rit. a tempo

-si-cian-ers you hear a-bout to-day, when the drums go bang, the cym-bals clang, the

horns will blaze a - way,___ Mac - Car - thy puffs the ould bas-soon while Doyle the pipes will

play; Oh! Hen-nes-sy Ten-nes-sy too-tles the flute, my word! 'tis some-thing grand, Oh! a

2. When - ev - er an e -
(Verse 3 see block lyric)

- lec - tion's on we play on ei - ther side._____ The way we play our

fine ould airs fills Ir - ish hearts with pride, oh! if poor Tom Moore was

liv - ing now, he'd make yez un - der - stand_____ that none could do him

Verse 3:
We play at wakes and weddings, and at ev'ry county ball
And at any great man's funeral we play the "Dead March in Saul"
When the Prince of Wales to Ireland came, he shook me by the hand
And said he'd never heard the like of "Macnamara's band."

Originally written in 1912, with lyrics added a year later, 'Memphis Blues' was the work of the so called 'father of the blues' William Christopher Handy and was used during the political campaign of a Memphis politician, William H. Crump. The song was featured in the films St Louis Blues (a biography of its composer) and Birth Of The Blues. The original lyrics to this song may be considered racially insensitive; however, they have been included for historical authenticity.

Memphis Blues

Words & Music by W. C. Handy

© Copyright 1913 Theron C. Bennett, USA.
© Copyright 1916 Assigned to Joe Morris Company, USA.
Campbell Connelly & Company Limited, 8/9 Frith Street, London W1.
All Rights Reserved. International Copyright Secured.

1. Hon - ey I've— been down, down to Mem - phis town, where the peo - ple smile

(Verse 2 see block lyric)

on you all— the while; hos - pi - ta - li - ty, they were good— to me,

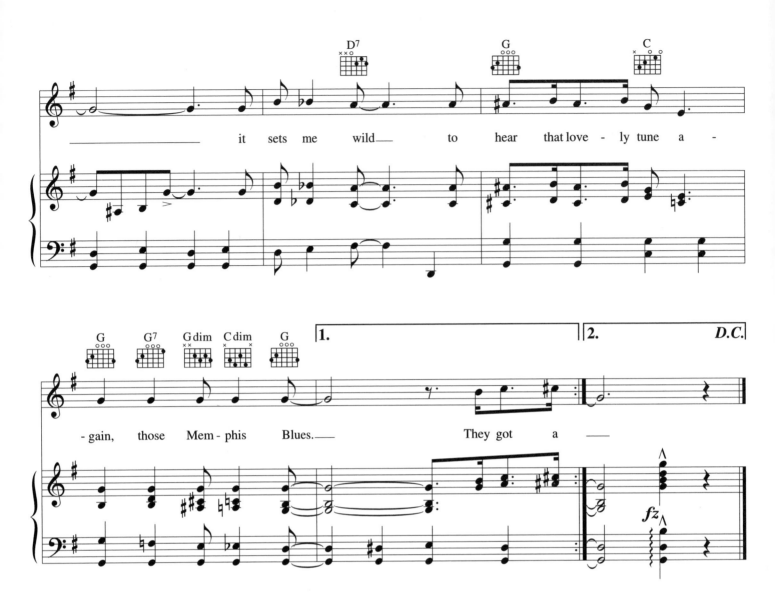

Verse 2:

Oh, that melody sure appeals to me
Like a mountain stream, flowing on it seem'd
Then it slowly died, with a gentle sigh
As the breeze that whines in the summer pines
Hear me people, hear me people, hear me, I pray
I'll take a million lessons till I learn how to play
Seems I hear it yet, simply can't forget, that blue refrain
There's nothing like the Handy Band
That plays the Memphis Blues so grand, oh them blues.

Moonlight Bay

Music by Percy Wenrich
Words by Edward Madden

© Copyright 1912 Remick Music Corporation, USA.
Redwood Music Limited, Iron Bridge House, 3 Bridge House, London NW1.
All Rights Reserved. International Copyright Secured.

Percy Wenrich from Joplin, Massachusetts started by playing in saloons and bars and sold his own self published compositions door-to-door. He subsequently wrote for many Broadway shows and married singer Dolly Connolly. He was 32 when he wrote one of his big hits 'Moonlight Bay', sung by Alice Faye in Tin Pan Alley and Doris Day in a film named for the song.

Verse 2:
Candle lights gleaming on the silent shore
Lonely nights, dreaming till we meet once more.
Far apart, her heart is yearning
With a sigh for my returning
With the light of love still burning
As in days of yore.

An early (1911) hit for American born
Nat D. Ayer was 'Oh! You Beautiful Doll',
which he wrote before coming to Britain,
in partnership with A. Seymour Brown.
It became the melody of car horns in the
1920s, was the title tune of a 40s film
and was danced to by Fred Astaire and
Ginger Rogers in the biographical film
The Story Of Vernon And Irene Castle.

Oh! You Beautiful Doll

Words & Music by Seymour Brown & Nat D. Ayer

© Copyright 1911 Remick Music Corporation, USA.
Redwood Music Limited, Iron Bridge House, 3 Bridge Approach, London NW1.
All Rights Reserved. International Copyright Secured.

Oh! you beau-ti-ful doll, you great big beau-ti-ful doll!

I love you so.

Let me put my arms a-bout you, I could nev-er live with-out you,

Oh! you beau-ti-ful doll, you great big beau-ti-ful doll! If you

Verse 2:
Precious prize, close your eyes
Now we're goin' to visit lover's paradise
Press your lips again to mine
For love is king of ev'rything.

Squeeze me, dear, I don't care!
Hug me just as if you were a grizzly bear
This is how I'll go thro' life
No care or strife when you're my wife.

Using the message of a famous war recruitment poster,
this song was also known as 'We Don't Want To
Lose You, But We Think You Ought To Go'.
Written by the famous London-born stage composer
Paul Rubens, it was later most effectively featured in
the stage musical Oh What A Lovely War and
memorably interpreted in the film version
by Maggie Smith.

Your King And Country Want You

Words & Music by Paul A. Rubens

© Copyright 1997 Dorsey Brothers Music Limited, 8/9 Frith Street, London W1.
All Rights Reserved. International Copyright Secured.

want you and miss you but with all our might and main we shall cheer you, thank you, * kiss you, when you come back a - gain. Oh! we don't want to lose you but we think you ought to go, for your King and your Coun - try both need you so; we shall

* When used for Male Voice substitue the word "bless" for kiss.

want you and miss you but with all our might and main we shall

cheer you, thank you, * kiss you, when you come back a - gain.

Verse 2:
We want you from all quarters
So, help us, South and North
We want you in your thousands
From Falmouth to the Forth
You'll never find us fail you
When you are in distress
So, answer when we hail you
And let your word be "yes"
And so your name, in, years to come
Each mother's son shall bless.

Encore Verse
It's easy for us women/people
To stay at home and home and shout
But remember, there's a duty
To the men who *first* went out
The odds against that handful
Were nearly four to one
And we cannot rest until
It's man for man, and gun for gun!
And ev'ry woman's/body's duty
Is to see that duty done!

* When used for Male Voices substitute the word "bless" for kiss.

A classic music hall song written for music hall star Lily Morris, who portrayed an indomitable char, by the reliable team of Clarles Collins and Fred Leigh. Many music hall stars refused to record their greatest hits, lest others copy them. Not so Lily Morris. She recorded her interpretation of the song both on film and gramophone record.

Why Am I Always The Bridesmaid?

Words & Music by Charles Collins & Fred W. Leigh

© Copyright 1917 Francis Day & Hunter Limited, 127 Charing Cross Road, London WC2.
All Rights Reserved. International Copyright Secured.

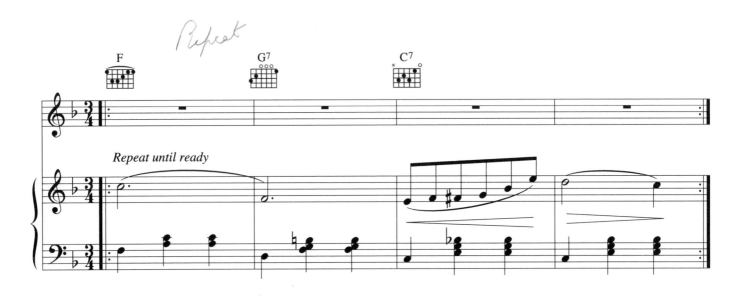

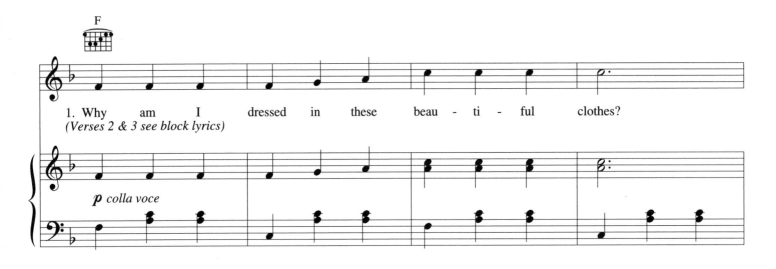

1. Why am I dressed in these beau-ti-ful clothes?
(Verses 2 & 3 see block lyrics)

What is the mat-ter with me?_____

I've been the brides - maid for twen - ty - two brides,

this time - 'll make twen - ty - three.

Twen - ty - two la - dies I've helped off the shelf,

no doubt it seemd a bit strange.

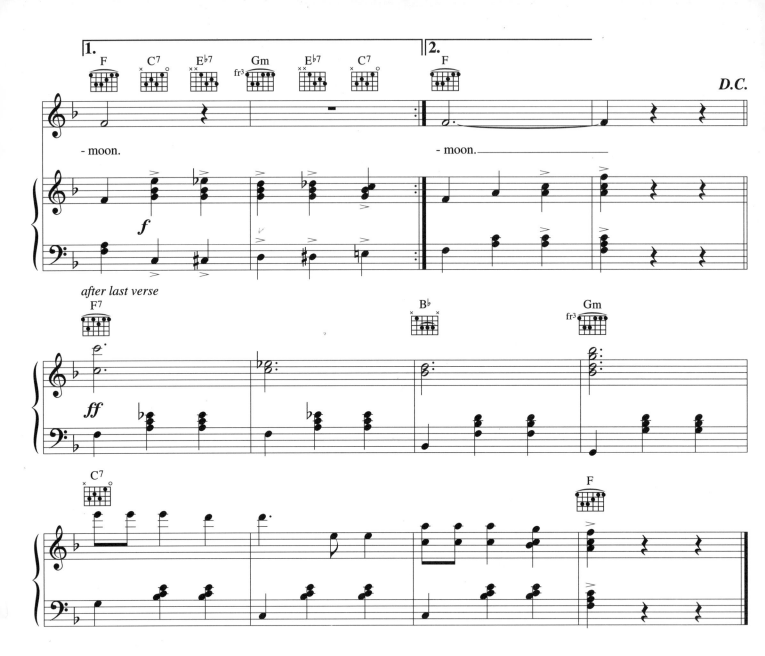

Verse 2:

Twenty-two times have I gone to the church
Followed the bride up the aisle
Twenty-two ladies have answered "I will"
Meaning "I won't" all the while.

Twenty-two couples I've seen go away
Just him and her on their own
Twenty-two times I have wished it was me
And gone back home to Mother alone.

Verse 3:

I had a good chance a week or two back
Took my young man home to tea
Mother got playful and gave him a pinch
Pinched my "financy" from me.

Being a widow she knew what to do
No use for me to complain
When they got married today, if you please
I was only the bridesmaid again.